LEARN ABOUT DYING WHEN YOU ARE NOT DYING

&

GRIEF & BEREAVEMENT

By

M. Kukreja, M.D.

LEARN ABOUT DYING WHEN YOU ARE NOT DYING

&

GRIEF & BEREAVEMENT

By

M. Kukreja, M.D.

Copyright © 2020

ISBN 9798218148294

Please note that this book uses the word "he" only for convenience. Everything applies equally to men and women as far as possible.

This book is dedicated to people everywhere.

"I felt that this book gave me peace of mind and an education on death."

Don Sebastian at Team Golfwell.

Emotions must never be fully expressed if you wish to control them; otherwise, they will control you.

If you do not go overboard in joy and anger, you will not go overboard in fear and sorrow.

This does not mean that you cannot cry and wail at the time of death. Of course, you can! However, you should not be swept away by your emotions. Similarly, the one who is "frozen" by her grief for months is completely enslaved by emotions! After some time, one should come into control.

Movies love to show us being swept away by emotions. But if they wish to portray realism, they should also depict the average person who has control over feelings instead of the impulsive one.

What you cannot allow your grief to do is to become destructive toward others or be self-destructive physically and emotionally (for example, in making decisions that you will regret later).

The one who is stoic in grief feels the pain as acutely as the one who is threshing on the ground.

Death and divorce do not mean that you break your relationships with the family of the deceased.

M. Kukreja

Contents

PREFACE 10

PART 1: HOW DO YOU INFORM OF A DEATH? 12
    CHAPTER 1: HOW TO INFORM OTHERS OF A DEATH 13

PART 2: BEREAVEMENT OF OTHERS 15
    CHAPTER 2: SHOULD YOU VISIT THE BEREAVED? 16

PART 3: DEATH IN GENERAL 22
    CHAPTER 3: DEATH, A MILESTONE 23
    CHAPTER 4: CHILDREN AND OTHERS 26
    CHAPTER 5: DEATH FROM COVID-19 28

PART 4: THE DYING 30
    CHAPTER 6: A FEAR OF DEATH 31
    CHAPTER 7: LISTEN TO SOMEONE DYING 33
    CHAPTER 8: YOUR DUTY TO THE DYING 36
    CHAPTER 9: WHEN YOUR LOVED ONE IS DYING 38
    CHAPTER 10: WHEN YOU ARE DYING 40
    CHAPTER 11: PLACE AND TIME OF DEATH 49

PART 5: SHOULD YOU TURN THE RESPIRATOR OFF? 52
    CHAPTER 12: WHEN TO TURN THE VENTILATOR OFF? 53

PART 6: AFTER DEATH 57
    CHAPTER 13: HOW TO TREAT THE DEAD 58

CHAPTER 14: CREMATION AND BURIAL 63

CHAPTER 15: AFTER DEATH 65

PART 7: GRIEF & BEREAVEMENT 67

CHAPTER 16: DO YOU NEED A "CLOSURE?" 68

CHAPTER 17: YOUR BEREAVEMENT 70

CHAPTER 18: HOW DO YOU HEAL? 75

CHAPTER 19: THE "DO-NOTS" OF GRIEF 78

CHAPTER 20: DO NOT BE IMPRISONED BY YOUR GRIEF 82

CHAPTER 21: BEREAVEMENT OF A SUICIDE 85

PART 8: BE STRONG 89

CHAPTER 22: YOUR MANTRA 90

CHAPTER 23: WHERE DO YOU GET YOUR STRENGTH? 91

CHAPTER 24: FACE YOUR DEATH 94

CHAPTER 25: THE MORAL RIGHTS OF A CHILD 96

PART 9: LEGAL ASPECTS OF DEATH 99

CHAPTER 26: A POWER-OF-ATTORNEY 100

CHAPTER 27: ORGAN DONATION 104

CHAPTER 28: ADVANCE DIRECTIVES 110

PART 10: THE MEDICAL PROFESSION 115

CHAPTER 29: HOW SHOULD A DOCTOR INFORM A DEATH? 116

CHAPTER 30: CRUELTY AND THE MEDICAL PROFESSION 120

PREFACE

If you are born, you must die.

Death is one of our milestones. Yet, while we handle joyous occasions, we do not know how to face sad times. Our religion and culture used to tell us what to do, but as more and more people have left their religion and as the State has cut down on our bereavement time, we are left to copy what the television shows us.

The television has become our teacher, whether endorsing an indecent dress code, being angry and violent, or being as rude as we can. This is sad because we forget that television is motivated by one thing alone, greed!

> The television is motivated by "what sells" and therefore is inappropriate for a teacher.

As a direct witness to deaths in my career as a physician, I have seen people face death in every possible way. I have seen people hit the dead body, curse it, or abandon it. I have seen mourners gossiping on their cellphones at a funeral giving attention to anyone else but the dead. *They conduct business deals at funerals.* These are not appropriate behavior. Neither is becoming frozen in grief or blaming your child over something he had no control over, like the death of his mother, or the fact that he resembles your deceased or ex-husband.

We must grow up!

This book is about how to treat the dying and how to handle death yourself. The fear in both situations is genuine. The fear is addressed in this book.

Grief cannot be handled by taking medication, drinking, running away, getting on a cruise, or remodeling your home. Grief can only be handled by facing it.

At the same time, we cannot let ourselves be imprisoned by our grief. There has to be a time limit for everything in this life.

Then we have to be set free to move on.

In today's world, we deal with leaving our instructions (advance directives) should we become unable to do so. We have to decide about organ donation. And, we have to be wary of losing our freedom when we give a "Power-of-Attorney" to others.

If we know the path to take, we have some comfort. If we prepare for death in advance, it will not be so fearful.

M. Kukreja, M.D.

PART 1: HOW DO YOU INFORM OF A DEATH?

CHAPTER 1: HOW TO INFORM OTHERS OF A DEATH

How do you inform the relatives of the death of their loved one?

Please do not tell the person over the phone.

It is highly non-caring of you and very traumatic to the loved one. If he happens to be walking down the stairs, he may fall upon hearing the news. If he is driving, he may have an accident. He may faint. He may have a heart attack.

If he then travels, his chance of an accident is very high. Go personally or send someone to meet the person and see that he is sitting when you break the news. Then stay with the person while he gets ready and bring him back with you or wait by his side until someone else arrives. The person is in shock and should not be left alone.

If you cannot go, inform someone close to him who can tell him. Someone should stay with him until all the travel arrangements are made and he is put on the train or plane. He should not drive. Someone should also be there to receive him.

This is caring and being humane!

How do you treat someone who has just learned of a death in his family?

People respond differently to death. Some may start screaming. Some may start crying. Even if they look calm, they may be in shock, or they may faint. Some may stay calm and handle it stoically.

When someone has learned of a death in his family, do not tell him to continue working, even if he is a doctor. Do not tell him to carry on with his daily routine, buying, cooking, etc. Understand that he is in shock.

He should not be alone. He should not be sent home alone. Someone should go with him. He needs to be safe while you take care of his needs and make decisions for him since he cannot. *This should be even if he appears to be in control.* Hold off legal decisions until he gets over his shock and better controls his grief.

PART 2: BEREAVEMENT OF OTHERS

CHAPTER 2: SHOULD YOU VISIT THE BEREAVED?

(Note: bereavement is being discussed earlier because you may have more occasions to go to a funeral than experiencing death personally).

If you care, you will be there.

The bereaved one has suffered a permanent loss. He is in shock, besides being overcome with grief. He needs some quiet time to digest this, but there is comfort in knowing that people are around and he is not alone. Do not speak to him if he does not wish to, but a touch, an embrace, or a squeeze of a hand shows that you care. The fact that you are there at this time means a lot.

You may miss a wedding, but you should not miss a death because that is where you and your caring are most needed. It is your duty to be at the funeral, visit the bereaved, and lend your support.

Those who say it is too painful, emotional, or scary to be there cannot be respected as grownups and must be considered selfish.

Whether you are a neighbor, relative, or friend, it is your duty to go to the funeral and home of the deceased. Never say that you are too upset to go and offer your condolences.

Strength, support, and comfort are of immense value. Do not just send a card or flowers, unless you are sick, out of the country, far away, or knew the deceased or the family only distantly.

Caring means giving your time.

It is selfish to check in at a hotel nearby, drinking and conversing with friends until it is time to attend the funeral.

It is also selfish to attend the funeral, then go somewhere for drinks and small talk, only to return to say goodbye to the bereaved when it is time to depart.

Stay a while.

It is non-caring to go to a funeral, partake in food, and then immediately go home or fly away, leaving the bereaved alone unless you were a mere acquaintance, did not know the family, and were only paying your respects.

As a relative, you must be prepared to spend some days after the funeral. You have to go to the deceased's home and be with the bereaved every step of the way.

What is the matter with us? Have we become so inhumane that we must return to our work and lives immediately? Is this how we show our love as relatives and friends? Rest assured that your work will continue without you if you drop dead tomorrow. This is about your character!

This is the time when the bereaved are most in shock and helpless. Your presence and time with them are mandatory. Go back to the bereaved's home and stay around. Your presence gives support! See what has to be done. Take over the chores and food.

Be prepared to give them two weeks! If you cannot do so, then take turns being there for at least 72 hours at a time for two weeks.

Take care of the bereaved.

Morality demands that you share the sorrow and offer your strength, support, and comfort, besides physical help, to a bereft person or a family overcome with pain for many weeks.

It is okay if you see anger instead of pain in the bereaved one's eyes. He is in shock. Do not say to the bereaved, "So you sent your father/spouse/child to another world," or "You drove him to it." Do not scold the bereaved.

This is not the time for the bereaved to be left alone. You should make arrangements among yourselves taking turns to stay with the bereaved for a period of two weeks. The rest should call him, members of the family, or friends daily to check if anything is needed or how they can help.

The well-wishers should bring food to the bereaved family daily for a week. There is a lot of physical and mental work to be done after death. Relatives, employers, employees, and others have to be informed. The dead person has to be cremated or buried. Rituals have to be performed and all legal formalities be completed. Certificates have to be obtained. Bank accounts have to be closed. The employer, beneficiaries, court, and lawyers have to be informed. Travel arrangements may have to be made. The employees, if any, have to be notified when they will be let go.

The bereaved should not do this alone. Do not let those grieving for the dead drive for two weeks. They are in shock and can get killed or kill someone. Friends and relatives are to be by his side. They have to take care of his work as he may be too distracted to think clearly. The relatives and friends are also dealing with grief. They must also be given a bereavement leave of three days by their employer to be with the family. They can take turns doing this.

Sit down for some time in the home of the one who died. Sometimes your presence alone can be comforting. Look around to see what chores you can take over. Take care of the phone calls if the family members are distraught. Go and get, or do, whatever is needed. Bring some food daily, or take turns, for one or two weeks.

Make sure the youngsters are taken out and distracted. Perhaps you can play with them. Pay attention to them. Give at least an hour to them, preferably more, while you are there. Go daily, or different members of your family can take turns for the next four weeks. It helps the bereaved to make the adjustment to his new life.

The soul is still around for the next few days. Pray with the bereaved. There should be daily prayers for the departed, followed by meals together for two weeks. Donate, however small, in his name. Or, do something good in his name.

Then visit the family once a week for the next two months. Friends can take turns on different days. If you are far away, make sure that you call every few days to see how the bereaved is doing for the next two months. This is called caring. This is social support.

On the first anniversary of the death, you should again be with the bereaved.

This must be a ritual where you pray for the departed and eat together. It is the "death anniversary meal."

Do not confuse this with a "party time." Fun and sadness do not mix.

Leave for bereavement.

Death is a terrible milestone that shakes our very foundation. To not understand this and for employers to insist that three to five days are sufficient for "bereavement leave" shows how cruel we have become. Bereavement leave should be for two weeks, at least.

It may take up to three months in the case of losing a child or a spouse. It takes that long to get one's balance back and to start working rationally without being obsessed with the one who died. It takes that long to deal with one's guilt, anger, and sorrow.

A struggling employer with a single employee should still give about three weeks of pay for the death of immediate relatives and three days to those attending the funeral. But he has a right to find another employee, even temporarily, if his business cannot survive. However, the government, and employers of over fifty employees, must give at least two weeks of paid leave and hold the position for two months.

PART 3: DEATH IN GENERAL

CHAPTER 3: DEATH, A MILESTONE

Death, like birth, marriage, and divorce, is a milestone.

Stand with respect when a dead person is passing by, regardless of what religion he belongs to. He is a human like you and is leaving your world. You owe him your respect.

Acknowledge that death is inevitable.

From the day you were born, it was known that you would die someday. It is unavoidable. Then why are you so unprepared for the death of your loved one? Do not be shocked and angry. Why are you looking to blame someone? Do not try to sue the doctors if your loved one dies an inevitable death. Do not take out your guilt on them. What are you looking for in a few more days? What more can you accomplish that you could not accomplish in a lifetime? Did you not have time to be together, to love, to talk, or to discuss plans?

Why are you angry at yourself? That you did not do enough? You did the best that you knew. Are you angry at the deceased for dying? He could not help dying. Are you angry that he did not take good care of his health? It was his right to live the way he pleased. Are you angry that he left you alone to face life's struggles alone? He could not help it. Do not lose faith in your capabilities.

Are you hostile to the medical profession for not having done enough? Even doctors cannot prevent themselves from dying when their time comes. Doctors can support the body to combat infection and breakdown, but they cannot prevent death, no matter how conscientious they are.

Are you angry at God for having taken your loved one away? Do you get angry when plants, animals, and other beings finish their life cycles? Do you not know that, if you are born, you will die? Do not fight death. Death is a natural process of life.

You have the pain of the separation, the anger at your fate, and the guilt for what you did or did not do. You need time, people, and work to recover. You need the faith that your loved one is on the other side. You must accept death as part of life.

Is this how the deceased would like you to live after he is gone? Would he like to see you so drowned in sorrow that you cannot think straight? Would he like to see you withdrawn and unable to function?

The departed one now knows that coming into this world means that we must live our lives to the fullest. We have to show our courage and learn to live, laugh, and love again. You can do so in his name! Live in a way that the departed is proud of you.

You cannot undo the past, but you can prevent it from controlling your future.

Find peace yourself.

Do not shun work and people. You will get your comfort from them. Keep in touch with your friends. You can be with them without discussing your loss.

If you cannot financially sustain yourself, you will not have peace.

Talk to your therapists, priests, or older and wiser people.

You will also be able to handle it if you consider this as part of your destiny.

Remember that "it is in giving that we receive." By helping others, we are helped. In this case, we receive comfort.

And it is in controlling our emotions that we become stronger.

CHAPTER 4: CHILDREN AND OTHERS

Children

Your children's grief is more painful. Their loss is far more acute. They have not yet learned coping skills. They do not have the same understanding, faith, or strength. Make sure they have someone to talk to and support them if you cannot. Do not neglect them. Just because they are quiet does not mean that they have no pain.

Children can view the body only if they are not afraid and are not alone. An adult should always be with them. Children under seventeen should not be taken to the burial or cremation. Small children should never be forced to kiss the dead or hug them. They can touch the dead, but only if they want to.

One should never blame a child for the parent's death. This is a sign of selfishness. Never make a child feel guilty for anyone's death.

One should never refuse to see a child because he or she reminds him of his spouse, who died or left.

You should never treat a child with anger because his other parent left you. It is not the child's fault. He is innocent, but you are being cruel and will suffer later in life. Be grateful that you have a child who is a part of you and who can give you such unconditional love.

Do not blame innocent children. It was you who caused their birth. Death does not entitle you to be selfish.

The widowed daughter-in-law

One of the cruelest things happens when you have a daughter-in-law who is financially dependent on you, and your son dies. This is critical when the daughter-in-law is uneducated.

This is the moment of truth when either your true cruel self will come forward, or you will show yourself to be human.

The moral rule is to treat your daughter-in-law in the same way as if your daughter had become widowed. You are to comfort and protect her. She is your daughter in the name of the law. Your home is hers. You must see that she has a monthly income to be spent with no questions asked. You must help her to get an education and so be able to support herself. You should treat her as you did when your son was alive.

You owe this to your son, who is watching from above!

But the immoral parents-in-law immediately blame the widowed girl for the death of their son proclaiming that she brought bad luck to him. They throw the daughter out or make her the unpaid servant of the house. They even lend her out for prostitution!

Such people belong in prison. They are the lowest of the lows. Their bank accounts should be impounded, and the court should see that a monthly income is given to the daughter-in-law as well as reasonable rent for the place she wants to stay at. She should not stay with her inlaws for the sake of her mental health.

CHAPTER 5: DEATH FROM COVID-19

With the pandemic of COVID-19 creating havoc, Many would learn of the death of their loved ones in hospitals and nursing homes but were not allowed to visit them before or after their deaths. This is tragic.

Unforeseen times bring unforeseen behavior. The goal of any epidemic *has to be to prevent the disease from spreading.* For this to happen, sometimes all acts of the formality and dignity of death, as we know it, are thrown out of the window.

In these difficult times, it helps to remember that we cannot choose our deaths, nor when and where we will die. The soldier who dies in the trenches or as a prisoner of war in the enemy territory is not surrounded by loved ones. His body is thrown into an unmarked grave. Does this mean that his loved ones suffer any less? Of course not!

The point to remember is this. Contrary to what the movies insist, *you do not need to see the body or know where it is to have closure.*

Do not add conditions to your grief.

When you are informed of the death of a loved one, grief starts surging in your heart. To add conditions by saying, "I need to be there," or "I need to see the body," (but the body is contagious or it is not possible) is to add agony and agitation to a mind already weighed down by deep sorrow.

The movies always make more money by making things more painful than they need to be.

Secondly, your agitation is not helping either the deceased or you. It does not matter that the body of the deceased is not in front of you. This is the time when you have to start your prayers and rituals for the deceased and his "peaceful transition" into the other world.

How can you pray for his peace when you are agitated?

The first rule is to accept that death has occurred. Accept the sorrow that has come.

The second rule is to embark on the death rituals just as if the deceased's body were in front of you.

Have the priest come into your home and recite prayers as he would have if he had been standing at the gravesite or the cremation site. If he has to do this outside your home or through facetime, so be it. Give your donations to the poor so that the deceased can have peace.

Read the chapter on grief.

Read the chapter "Do you need closure?"

Promise the deceased that you will take care of his loved ones. Do something in the name of the deceased. And strive for peace for yourself.

PART 4: THE DYING

CHAPTER 6: A FEAR OF DEATH

People react very differently when they learn that they are dying. Some may be overcome with terror. Some may be in sorrow because they can no longer take care of those dependent upon them. Some may be in denial. Some may be depressed. Some will receive the news calmly.

This is, despite the fact, that the one thing that we know for sure from the day that we were born is that we will die! Yet, we see people dying, and we feel sorry for them. Why? We run around and blame doctors when someone dies as if one were supposed to live forever!

Death is frightening to most people. It strikes one with awe to see someone who is interacting with people and then becomes a mechanical piece, nonreactive and decaying very quickly. It matters not how passionate or powerful he had been. It matters not whether he was poor or rich, powerful or humble, caring or cruel. The end is the same. It is truly one of the miracles of life!

But the idea that we lose our identity and physical contact with our loved ones on earth, is what makes us tremble.

It is frightening that we must leave this world and everything we know in it and travel to a destination that no one returns to describe.

For each of us, it is an unknown journey with no guidelines.

Let us discuss our fear

We are scared because we do not want to become "nothing."

But we will not become "nothing" on dying. We will retain our identity.

We are scared because of the unknown.

But we are going back to where we came from.

We are scared that we will be abandoned and alone.

But we will be surrounded by loved ones.

We are scared that we will lose contact with our loved ones.

But we will be able to watch over them.

When our loved ones are gone, we think that they have turned into dust, and the finality of that loss is overwhelming.

Many doctors have seen evidence of the afterlife as they deal with the dead and dying. Some good books to read are "On Life After Death," by Dr. Elisabeth Kubler Ross, and the books by Dr. Raymond Moody.

Many a person will tell you of feeling the presence of his departed one and even being protected by him. It is comforting to know this when our loved ones leave us and when we leave this earth.

Do not be frightened. You are merely stepping into the next world. Your intelligence, personality, and your soul will not die. You will be met with familiar people.

CHAPTER 7: LISTEN TO SOMEONE DYING

Do not be in denial with those dying.

If someone who has been ill says that he is dying, you should not say, "Do not talk like that. You are fine." He is not a fool. We know when our time has come. Do him the courtesy of listening to him. Time is running out, and he desperately needs to talk with someone before it is too late, whether it is his last wishes, instructions, the need to absolve feelings of guilt, or communicating other thoughts.

It does not make you look cold or heartless. Nor will it make you hasten his death if you acknowledge that he is dying.

If he says he is dying, say, "Do you think so? Is there something that I can do to comfort you?" What can I do to help? Is there something I can get you? Would you like to talk about something?" Listen to his thoughts and final wishes. Take care of his worries. Help him to take care of his affairs and his wishes. If the dying person wishes to acknowledge death, you, as the relative, should not deny death or refuse its pain. Do not pretend that everything is fine.

The patient, especially if a child, generally knows. It is a burden for the dying child to lie to his parents and see his parents lie to him. You do not have to tell a child that he is dying. But if he asks, you can tell him that he will be going to his other home where his relatives are (who are already dead), and who, like the angels, will look after him until you join him. Tell him that, like the caterpillar who changes his form to become a butterfly, he is changing his form (Read Dr. Kubler-Ross, a physician and the author of books on death and dying).

Fear of death is a real fear.

Fear of death is a real fear to many. You can say that you want no resuscitation in your will, but when the moment comes and one is facing death, many people will change their minds and want full resuscitation.

It is here that the tragic drama begins. The family member, or perhaps the nurse, who is in a hurry or has already made her own decision about the patient, will decide that the patient is too confused to know what he is saying and will not grant him the right to change his mind. "Why did he write *no resuscitation* when he was not sick?" she asks. Surely, he must be confused.

Is it a crime to change one's mind? Do we not all change our minds? Why should you call us confused when we do so? If we decided to go inside a lion's den and changed our mind upon seeing the lion, who would blame us for doing so?

It is so very wrong not to give him the right to change his mind.

Not having faced death themselves, the nurses and the relatives have no idea what the terminal patient is going through. Ethics demands that if the patient changes his mind, and the doctor understands this, no one can refuse the patient his wish.

Do not leave a dying patient alone.

Listen to a dying person if he says that he is afraid of being alone. Take turns sitting near a dying person for at least a few hours daily, so that somebody is with him around the clock. Talk to him. Read to him. Ask him if he needs something. Wipe his face. Give him a sip of water. Hold his hand. Pray with him. If he is waiting for a relative who is not able to make it in time, be that relative. Fill in his place.

Make sure that one person or another is with him. This is very important. Some people are afraid of death, and it is so tragic to see them lying alone and terrified in their rooms. It is inhumane. As long as there are relatives and friends, they must do this for the patient.

There must be a leave granted for seven days to attend to those who are dying. Read the scriptures to the dying person even though he is in and out of consciousness. The soul can hear. Pray near him. But step away periodically to refresh, and take care of yourself.

Hospitals should have a person to sit by the dying patient if he has no one.

CHAPTER 8: YOUR DUTY TO THE DYING

Visit the dying.

Someday when you die, you will not wish to die alone.

When a person is dying, he should have visitors. Like the rest of the book, this applies to both men and women. To say that you are uncomfortable seeing your relative/friend dying, and so are not visiting him, or not allowing him to come home to die for this reason, shows how selfish and immature you are. It does not show your love for him.

And someday, you will be treated the same way!

This is about your personal development. This is basic humanity as it is practiced in the rest of the world. To be human, you have to accept all the aspects of life, not just those that give you pleasure. So never say that you cannot handle this. Say, "I must handle this with caring." To refuse to go because he may think that you are feeling sorry for him is another crazy notion.

It is not about what anyone thinks. It is about doing what is right.

No alcohol.

When you visit the ill, the dying, or the dead, do not drink alcohol. *Do not use a crutch!* Show respect to them by being in your full senses.

Do not fight

Do not fight in the vicinity of the dying. This is not the time to fight with each other or to bring out the bad points of the one dying. This is not the place to be selfish and only think about yourself. If you want to fight, go far away to do so.

When you visit

By being with the dead or dying, you show love or respect for him and his family members. Go and offer your condolences. Let them cry on your shoulder. Give what help you can.

Do not refuse to see the dying person because he is in the house of someone you dislike. Grow up.

If you were upset with the deceased, this is not the time to speak ill of him to others. Even if you are not talking to the bereaved, have the grace to extend your condolences to them. Your development demands this.

There is no room for anger or arrogance in death.

CHAPTER 9: WHEN YOUR LOVED ONE IS DYING

Do not start acting as if the loved one is already gone, and disassociate yourself from him while he is still alive. This is a very selfish and cruel behavior.

When your loved one is dying, your life will be completely disrupted at this time. While you make sure that the children follow their routine as much as possible, you should see that the dying person gets priority. Children, too, have to learn the skills and protocol involved in a death. Let them visit him as much as possible. If they ask whether he is dying, acknowledge that there is such a possibility. Answer their questions.

What about you?

You should have a pastor or friend to talk to. Arrange for someone to take care of your loved ones if you need some time to handle your pain or strengthen yourself. You may feel numb or feel a choking sensation. You may be overcome with guilt, anger, shock, and disbelief. You may not hear what the doctor or nurse says, so ask someone else to be with you. Please do not drive a vehicle at this time and even for two weeks after the death. Pray for strength. Pray that your loved one has strength.

Festivals

Do not celebrate birthdays, other happy occasions, or festivals when a family member is dying. Your child is then being shown that his joy is more important than the impending loss and current grief. *This is how you make a selfish child.* When the family grieves, the child grieves.

This is not about "life has to go on." This is about teaching your children to handle death and the dying, a milestone.

Your child should be told that his birthday or occasion will be celebrated another time since the family member is not well. This shows the child that you care and respect the one dying, and so should he.

No festivals should be celebrated during the dying and in the next three months after the death. You can donate some food, clothing, or money to the poor on such occasions in the dead person's name. Any marriage should be postponed for three months unless all arrangements have already been paid for.

There must be time for grief.

CHAPTER 10: WHEN YOU ARE DYING

Please note that this has nothing to do with committing suicide. The reader is referred to the book "Emotional Pain versus Suicide" by the author to deal with suicide.

How will you react when you are dying? Death, like birth, is one milestone that you have to go through alone. It is one milestone that no one can come back and leave guideposts for you to follow.

All around us, we hear that people are dying, yet we cannot come to grips with our own mortality. And this is regardless of how educated we are or how responsible a position we may hold. All our experiences do not seem to prepare us for death. Why?

Do you not know that death occurs at any time and at different times to different people? Did not your parents or grandparents die before you? Do animals not accept death? It is important that we, daily, have a fleeting acceptance that we will die and that this is the rule of life.

Death has become a taboo subject, leaving everyone to their own device to cope with it.

But we must talk about it. We must figure out the best way to handle this, our most significant milestone.

Fear of dying

Read about our fears in the chapter, "A Fear of Death."

You have a choice of being overcome with terror or sitting down and facing the facts of life. Ask yourself why you are falling to pieces. Are you afraid of turning into nothing? You are not. Are you afraid of the unknown? Try substituting curiosity for fear. Do you want to be around longer? It is not in your hands, and all your crying is not going to make it happen.

You are like a babe who cries in the womb and is afraid to come out because it does not know of life! You are afraid because you know not of death and what is ahead of it.

You are not turning into dust by dying.

You are still "you" with all your traits and personality who will now embark on a new journey. You can see and hear just as you do now. You cannot die. It is the body that dies. You will go forward.

You will not die alone.

Beings who have died before you and those from the other world will come to accompany you.

Yes, miracles happen. Yes, a new drug may appear on the market. And you may be saved. That is wonderful!

But in the interim, it is also true that if you do not run around in fear, you may have more strength to handle life. If you do not run around in fear, you may enjoy your remaining life with a new perspective.

We cannot control our way of birth. But we can control the way we die.

Emotions

The most common emotions near death are fear, anger, sorrow, regret, and the realization that you have made many mistakes. But one also sees a dead person frozen with an expression of anger at the time she left this life.

Do not be angry because you are dying. We come to this earth to overcome our bad tendencies. Anger is one of them.

If you have conquered anger in this life, you have achieved a milestone.

Some dying people are peaceful. They have led a good, fulfilling life, did what they wanted to do, or did the best they could in their circumstances. Some people are dying in fulfillment of their duty as in defending someone and accepting this. The key word is acceptance.

> Acceptance is important.
> Leaving yourself in God's hands is important.
> Asking for strength from Him is important.
> Praying is important.

Acceptance does not mean that you turn your face to the wall, feel sorry for yourself, and refuse to talk to your family. If you do so, you lose your last chance to climb up another step of the development ladder. This is your final chance to pull out your courage and show the rest of us how to die in friendliness, peace, and acceptance.

Things to do while you have the time.

Physically, try to do something for yourself every day, even if it is to sit up by yourself or feed yourself. If you have more strength, you can do your activities of daily living. You can walk around in your room.

Mentally, it is time to see that your affairs are in order so there will be no confusion left behind. It is a wise person who has his affairs organized at his death. Finish whatever projects you can. Read the book that you have always wanted to read.

Emotionally, you still have some time to learn. Can you let go of the bitterness, hatred, anger, and fear inside you? Is it worthwhile to still stay angry inside? You do not have to talk to the person you are angry at, but you can stop being angry at him. If you wish to mend fences, this is your chance.

Like any emotion, anger is a blanket that covers you so that intelligence cannot get through.

Death is a time when you want your intelligence intact as long as possible. So, let go of your anger. For the same reasons, avoid drugs like morphine as far as possible.

Socially, be willing to meet people. You do not have to say much. A nod or a smile is fine. You will want to be alone at times to get back your strength. We understand that.

Spiritually communicate with your Maker. Tell him of your fears and your regrets. Ask for peace and forgiveness.

Would you like to help someone around the time of your death? See if you can make the last donation to the poor or the animals before you leave or leave that in your will. It gives one peace. Call it getting a "last-minute credit!"

Do not waste your time.

Do not waste this time with mundane topics when you talk to someone. Speak of your regrets, your wishes, and your concerns. Reassure the loved ones you choose of your love and forgiveness. When you feel weak, of course, let the others know. They can still sit by you and read or talk softly among themselves.

You are embarking on a journey.

Like any journey that you undertake, you should prepare for the journey of death. You can finally put away all pretense and lies and be honest with yourself and others.

Put your affairs in order. Remove the unnecessary stuff that you have accumulated.

Make your will. That should not be known to others until after your death.

Decide if it is possible to die where you want to. It might be your home.

Decide if there is anyone you want to talk to or repair relations with.

If possible, go wherever or do whatever makes you happy.

How should you act?

You cannot control dying, but you can control your living till the end of your strength.

Speak to people as long as you have the strength to do so.

Be interested in the news until you no longer can.

Remain curious for as long as you can.

Be willing to learn as long as you can. Your knowledge goes with you.

Be friendly and interested in other people for as long as you physically can. If people around you are too busy rushing around to talk to you, it is their loss. They are losing their chance to develop compassion while facing another's death. Turn to your books and memories, and talk to the angels.

Do not turn your face to the wall.

When you are dying, do not turn your face to the wall and refuse to interact with people. It is one thing to withdraw because you are tired. It is another thing if you do so because you are angry at life or are depressed. It is all right to shed your tears. You feel helpless. But know the following.

You have one more lesson to teach the rest of us, and that is how to die. If you keep an interest in the world around you and keep interacting with others, as long as you have the strength to do so, you will not be burning in pain and sorrow inside. You will have peace, and the spark of life in you will burn brighter till the end.

Would you like to meet someone? Would you like to eat a particular dish? If there is something you want to eat, you can have it. What harm can be done? You are dying anyway. Would you like to hear some hymns, prayers, or pop music? If you do not, that is fine too. Would you like to go somewhere that is possible to go? Would you just like to touch or hold a hand? When you wish to be left alone, we will honor it.

Let us now prepare.

Most of us would like to die fully alert until the last minute. Let your relatives and the nurse know that. They should honor your wishes and not force you to have morphine to make you unconscious in your last hours.

Tell the hospice nurse not to dope you with morphine until you tell her to do so. It must be active permission, not just a grimace that you make. Too many people are doped needlessly just because they grimaced. A hospice nurse should never do that.

If you are anxious, you should consciously concentrate on your breathing and try to make it slow and deep instead of rapid and fast. It is comforting to hold someone's hand as you do so.

Do two things:

Let go and be in peace. Leave yourself in God's Hands.

Tell God that you are putting yourself in His hands. Do not be afraid when you die. You leave a worn-out body to go on a new adventure. Focus in front of you and say God's name. Say, "I am in Your hands."

Divine Light

You will see many sights and hear different sounds after death. Do not be distracted by them.

But you will also see this Divine Light. Focus on the Light and follow it. Our love and prayers will surround you.

For the relative/friend

You, too, will be traveling this path in the future.

The dying is frightened of loneliness. Have somebody stay with the person around the clock.

Do not be in denial about the dying.

If he says that he is dying, do not say, "You are fine!" He knows when he is dying. Instead, say, "Do you think so? What can I do to help? Is there something I can get you? Would you like to talk about something?"

Do a task for the dying daily.

It may be only to wipe his face with a cool cloth, change his water, read to him or sit beside him for an hour, and so on. He will let you know what he wants.

This is not the time for you to show your impatience, bitterness, anger, greed, or non-caring!

Pray with the dying.

Pray any prayer that he wishes.

Pray for the dying.

You can say: "Our love is with you. May you go in peace. May the Lord take you in His hands."

CHAPTER 11: PLACE AND TIME OF DEATH

Place of death.

Where would you like to die? Will it be in a cold, lonely place where strangers hurry in and out, according to their shifts? Or would you prefer your home in familiar surroundings, surrounded by loved ones? Think about this when you decide where your loved one should die.

One of the saddest situations is when a hospital transfers a dying patient to another facility because this is what the insurance company demands. For a person to be sent to another strange place as he lies helpless and dying is the ultimate non-caring. This cruelty is caused by the insurance company. The insurance company will only pay if the dying patient is transferred to a strange place.

Death should be a peaceful experience for the person involved. As far as possible, it should be at home or in familiar surroundings with loved ones around. The dying person has a right to die at home. But this is being denied to the patient, as the family frantically insists on keeping him in the hospital. The family does so, hoping that the loved one may live a day or two longer in the hospital.

Why? You had a lifetime! What are a few more isolated days in a hospital with needles and tubes compared to death at home surrounded by loved ones? Do not deny that to him. However, if the patient needs medical care until the end, nursing that you cannot provide, or if you are away from home, then this is understandable.

Time of death.

When one's loved one is dying, it is the family's right to be with the dying person in terminal cases or where no resuscitation is being done. All hospitals must arrange for this.

But, the family should not be present while resuscitation is being done. Leave the doctors to work with full concentration.

Do not force your children to be near if they are scared. They can wait outside the room. Hold your loved one's hand as he departs. Ask if there is something that he wants you to take care of.

Tell him that you love him. Say, "Take God's name. Leave everything in God's hands. Look for the Light as you go and follow It. Go in peace. May God be with you. Our love is with you. We will meet again."

Sometimes a dying person cannot speak. But you can talk to him. Touch or hold him. Say that you love him and that you are putting him in God's hands and His love. If your loved one is afraid and asks for medical attention, send for medical help, and ask your loved one to say God's name. Your presence is comforting.

Insurance companies have no business taking over the medical profession in this country, yet they have done so, which profoundly affects medical care. It is time that they were stopped. Insurance companies dictate everything, including how doctors should treat their patients, what medicines they can give their patients, and how long they can keep their patients in a hospital. That itself should be grounds for malpractice.

It is time that Congress created a board made of doctors and lay people to oversee the activities of insurance companies.

Insurance companies care only about money, not about the patients' needs. Check out how much a CEO of an insurance company makes. Look at the huge buildings they have put up, and yet they do not want to pay for patient care and dictate what care the patients can receive and where they will die.

PART 5: SHOULD YOU TURN THE RESPIRATOR OFF?

CHAPTER 12: WHEN TO TURN THE VENTILATOR OFF?

Sometimes, we have to make the heartbreaking decision to turn off the "life-support" machine that our relative is on. But we feel so guilty that we cannot. We feel that we are killing our relative! We need clarity of vision about this.

SIX QUESTIONS NEED TO BE ASKED

If you love this person, you will ask only six questions:

1. Can my loved one recover?

2. Is this the quality of life he would want to have in his final days?

3. Am I causing suffering to the person by keeping him attached to the respirator?

4. Am I prolonging the agony of death?

5. Am I taking away his right to die in dignity and peace?

6. Would I like to live like this, day after day, before I die?

Death is the natural result of life. Everyone has to die. We must accept this.

The patient is already gone. It is the respirator, other technology, or medications that are keeping the body alive.

He is alive only as long as he is tied to a machine, unable to move for more than a few inches, do anything he wants, communicate, laugh, and make daily decisions for himself. He is completely dependent on others. He cannot even turn in bed by himself.

Is this how you would wish to spend the last few days of your life?

Is this kindness to make a dying person suffer the last few days like this? He is going to die eventually. Will you prolong his agony just so that you can see him open and shut his eyes? Does that make sense? Would you like to die such a miserable death tied to a machine? No one would want additional suffering before his death, and you are prolonging the suffering by not stopping the machine.

We would willingly stay like this for days or weeks tied to a machine if we then recovered and could function again as ordinary human beings.

Do not prolong the agony of death.

The purpose of life support (the respirator and medications) is to give the body time so that it can recover and get well again.

But if the body cannot recover, then the respirator is never to be used to prolong the dying process.

Life support makes a person a helpless creature completely dependent on others for every movement, breath, food, water, and passing urine. This is to be tolerated only if it is a temporary measure, and there is a chance of recovery. But we must not have false hopes. If an animal were thus suspended immobile, you would say it was cruelty. Yet somehow, when our relative or friend is on a respirator, we are scared to say it is time to stop. We feel that we are the one who is killing him. This is not true.

He has already begun the dying process.

By keeping the respirator, we are prolonging death and making it painful.

Life means acting, reacting, and interacting consciously.

We are to let the soul free as it was meant to be free. If he is in a coma and there is no hope, you have to release him to enter another world. If the car is broken down, you do not insist on driving it. You do not wish to stay trapped in it.

You are not murdering him by taking him off the respirator.

He is dying anyway. Once two doctors have documented that nothing more can be done to make the patient recover, then you must stop the respirator and let him go with minimal suffering and with dignity.

Do not attach someone to a respirator so that he lies there day after day, waiting for death.

You attach him to a respirator only to see if this will help him to recover.

Remember that death is a natural outcome of our lives. Stop the machine. Let him die a natural death, free and not hooked to anything. Free the soul to move on. You can ask that the patient be given pain medications so that he is comfortable. That does not mean that he is to be sedated until he dies. We all wish to keep our senses alert before we leave. If he asks, you can give him whatever he wishes for, including water. But you do not have to give him intravenous fluids for hydration. There is not much hydration needed when one is dying. Do not have him fed through artificial means, through the nose, a PEG tube, or intravenously.

Stop all tests that will not change the dying process.

Sit and take turns reading holy books to him or saying prayers. But suppose he is an atheist. Then listen to his wishes to stop the prayers. Hold his hand and say, " Take my strength." And give him your time and care.

(Author's note: The chapters on Advance Directives and Organ Donation are in the latter part of this book).

PART 6: AFTER DEATH

CHAPTER 13: HOW TO TREAT THE DEAD

Immediately after death, the soul is still around. Immediate relatives should be left alone with the dead for a while to say their final words to him. This should be done in the hospital or at home if the death occurred at home. Those, other than the immediate family, can stay outside while this is being done. Before they do this, all the people in the room should say a small prayer. You can say a prayer that you know. If you cannot think of one, you can say, "We pray for you. May God be with you. We love you very much." If people are too dazed to say this, they should not be forced to.

Teenagers

Teenagers should not be left alone with the deceased right after his death unless they request it. They need an adult, a nurse, a relative, or a friend just to stand quietly nearby. This person can comfort them if they become overwhelmed or tell them what to do if they are dazed or in shock. It is comforting for them to know that they are not alone in their grief. If they want to kiss or hug the deceased, they can do so, but they should not be forced to do anything.

Alcohol and medicines

Do not drink alcohol to handle your loss or take sedatives or other psychiatric medication. It only hides the pain. It does not destroy the pain. *The minute you stop the medicine, the pain comes back.* Why did it come back? Why did the medicine not eradicate it? It cannot. It can only block the pain. Yet, by handling this emotion, you would be able to destroy it.

What one does not do!

You do not shake the dead, hit him, and say, "Get up." Do not scold him or rant and rave at him. Do not shout at him, "How can you leave me? How could you do this to me?" That shows selfishness and anger instead of sorrow. He had no control over this! It is enough that you shed your tears.

Anger has no place in death.

Stay with the loved one for some time after he is gone. Put your arms around him. Be silent if you cannot speak what is in your heart.

Cultural preferences

Cultural preferences must always be respected. Some cultures want the body to lie on the floor for a few minutes (*Dust unto dust*). Unless the deceased was contagious, they should be allowed to do so. The dead cannot be further damaged. If requested by the family, the deceased should be allowed to return to his home for a final farewell in his familiar surroundings. This, of course, can only happen if the home is nearby.

Show respect for the dead.

The dead body must be treated with the utmost respect. It should never be allowed to lie exposed, naked. Close the eyes of the dead person. The dead body should not be treated as a contagious being whom you loathe to touch. It belonged to your loved one. It should be bathed by the family members as a sign of caring and put in clean clothes. Why do you wait for outsiders to come and bathe your loved one? Can you not do that much for him?

Many people do not know how to behave at a funeral place.

There are four rules:
1. Give your full concentration.
There is to be no looking at your cell phones, making calls, or gossiping.

2. Dress and behave with dignity.

3. Show respect for the deceased. Talk in soft tones.

4. The fourth rule is to shut off your cell phones.

No cell phone should be used in a funeral place. If you have to make an urgent call, go outside the funeral place to do so.

Do not conduct your business during a funeral. This is very disrespectful. Shut your phone off.

When you are in the place where the dead body is lying, show respect for the deceased. Do not laugh and joke. Do not talk loudly. Do not smoke, drink alcohol, or chew gum.

Do not wear makeup. Do not dress immodestly. Do not wear tight clothing. Do not dress in shorts. Do not show your breasts, cleavage, thighs, or buttocks. Do not wear shorts. Respect your culture and dress accordingly. Some will wear black or white as their custom is.

Give your condolences to the family and sit down quietly for some time. "Quietly" means that you do not use your cell/mobile phones in the place of death. Show that much respect for the dead. Pray quietly for the dead.

A place of death is not a battleground.

Do not prevent estranged relatives or people you have fought with from coming and paying their respects or walking with the deceased's procession. It is their right, no matter how much they may have fought with you or the deceased. Do not stop them from seeing the dead person. Open the cover on the face of the deceased for them unless the deceased was highly disfigured by an accident.

Do not fight with them or glare at them. Do not raise points of contention at this time. Greet them quietly at this time. Treat them with courtesy. Offer them some water or food if they have come from far. Do not accuse a person of wishing the deceased dead. We all say things that we do not mean in anger, but it is cruelty to remind one at such a time.

This is neither the time nor place to bring up bitterness, fights, or recriminations.

You must not stop people from visiting the dead even if they were not on talking terms with them. They still have the right to pay their respects. This may be their chance to come to peace with the dead.

However, if the deceased clearly expressed his wishes that certain people not attend his funeral, then his wishes must be respected.

Children

The children must not be neglected. Someone must talk to them about their loss and comfort them. Someone must distract them and see that they are fed and taken care of. They are also dealing with tremendous pain and shock. It is important to designate one or two persons for this.

A divorced person

People should understand that a divorced person, too, can feel intense pain and grief at the loss of a former spouse. The futility of what could have been and what was wasted, the despair of what was destroyed, the pain of all those years, the unfairness of it all, and the finality of it all are emotions pouring through. Or, there may be guilt, anger, or non-caring.

CHAPTER 14: CREMATION AND BURIAL

Hindus who cremate their dead, must not waste milk by pouring it over statues or objects during prayer. This is so shameful!

It is cruel to the cow, who could have fed its young, and it is cruel to a human being to waste milk this way. It is far better if you feed a hungry child with that milk.

A religion cannot be associated with cruelty.

Cremation or burial should be done within the week. Burial has to follow your protocol. Ashes should be disposed of within a week unless a loved one has to come from far away or you have to take the ashes far. In that case, they should still be disposed of within a month. This is respect. The deceased does not become a commodity that you can dispose of at your convenience.

Any "religious act" that has cruelty is immoral and cannot be followed.

Do not ask that your pets be killed when you die. This is inhumane. If you have no one willing to take care of your pets, call the rescue societies. Never burn or bury a living person or an animal with the deceased as part of the ceremony!

Also, do not make anything out of silver and give it to your priest so that your loved one can safely cross over to heaven. This is a gimmick made up by greedy priests. According to this logic, no poor person can go to heaven.

Are you trying to bribe the Gods?

But it will bring peace to the deceased if you feed the animals and the poor in his name and give them clothing. This should also be done every year on his death anniversary.

CHAPTER 15: AFTER DEATH

The soul does not leave immediately. Every day for two weeks after the funeral, perhaps you and your relatives or friends can gather in the evening before dinner to say a prayer for the deceased. Do not force the children, spouse, or parent to do this if it is too painful for them to do so. You can say it for them. You can choose any prayer that you wish. For those who do not know of any prayer for the dead, you can say the following:

"Go in peace. Our love is with you.
Please forgive us as we forgive you.
May God be with you."

Find peace for the deceased and yourself.

Do three things:

First, *promise* the deceased that you will do something constructive to bring him peace. This usually means taking care of those he left behind or of something that he left unfinished.

It never means revenge! He has risen above revenge in the next world.

Second, *do something* in the name of the deceased. It can be anything, including a donation to a charity or helping someone in his name.

Third, *find peace* yourself.

Understand that the deceased, too, needs peace. If he looks down and sees you in emotional pain, he cannot have peace either. For his sake, and your own sake, it is vital that you get control of your emotions.

Come to your baseline temperament within a few months.

Let us pray. We say:

> May you have peace where you have gone,
>
> May I have peace, who is left behind,
>
> I forgive you for any pain that you caused me.
>
> Please forgive me for any pain that I caused you.
>
> My love will always be with you,
>
> I shall help someone so that you may have peace,
>
> I shall give to a charity that you may have peace,
>
> I shall pray to God that we both have peace.

PART 7: GRIEF & BEREAVEMENT

CHAPTER 16: DO YOU NEED A "CLOSURE?"

People have falsely invented the term "closure." Like any idea that allows conditions to be put forth *before we accept responsibility,* it has spread like wildfire.

First, let us be clear about what we mean by the term "closure." Death is a fact of life. To say that you will not have closure unless you see the dead body means that *you will not accept the death of a person.*

However, one cannot deny the fact that he is dead!

Second, all over the world, people are killed in wars, natural disasters, illnesses like COVID-19, and in far-away prisons. They are not seen by their loved ones. Their loved ones accept their death. It is entirely up to you if you wish to be in denial and refuse to accept the death.

But you are the one who will have no peace!

In Hindu and Buddhist customs, the bodies are cremated in the same spot, one after another. The ashes are then deposited in the river to be washed away. There is no hallowed spot that belongs to one's loved one. This is to remove attachment to the place of death. The ashes are not kept since the soul should not stay attached to this earth.

That does not mean that they suffer from a lack of closure or grieve any less.

Third, if you think that by seeing the body or knowing where the body is, you will stop having pain and become peaceful, think again! If you think that you can now forget about the person and get along with your life, you could not be more wrong!

There is no door in your brain that you can shut upon a milestone and walk away. The movies are a lie.

Whether you see the body or not, the pain and despair will remain for a long time, years.

When you say that you have no closure, it means that you are not at peace. However, you would not be at peace even if you saw the body. So why put forth conditions? You will not be at peace for a very long time.

It is not about *where* the person was killed, *where* he lies after death, or *whether* his body was seen after death. What should matter is that the person is dead.

There should be no conditions with milestones of birth and death.

CHAPTER 17: YOUR BEREAVEMENT

The memory of the one we lost is so painful. Our chest feels as if it will burst from the pain. Nothing makes sense. The loneliness, the ache, the sharp pain, and the heaviness inside seem so much to bear that we sometimes cannot breathe. It is as if someone has ripped our hearts out of their place.

People react differently depending on their personalities and how life has treated them. Then there are immediate reactions and later reactions.

Immediate Reactions

One cannot stop wailing. All activities of daily living stop.

One may go into shock and not understand what is being said to him, forget to eat and drink, and be unable to participate in daily activities.

An abused person may have Stockholm's Syndrome and, therefore, will go into shock or have no coping strength because of her dependency on the deceased.

One may be frozen into silence or withdraw into a corner.

One may become angry and hostile to others and God.

One may have panic attacks and feel that he cannot handle life. He may feel that he is falling apart.

One may be overcome with guilt.

One may become suicidal. He feels that life is no longer worth living.

Or, one may accept what has happened and, with all his pain, grief, and loss, still be able to take care of himself and others.

This is true in poorer countries when survival is at stake or other children are involved. But even in the United States, Lincoln, despite the death of his child and a half-crazed wife, led the nation successfully through the Civil War.

And despite the death of his son and his imprisonment, Mandella persevered in the struggle for the freedom of his nation.

Neither shouted nor acted angrily and violently!

Remember this when the television tells you to react by shouting, fighting, being angry, and being destructive.

That is wrong.

You are not a slave to your emotions. You are their master.

There are countless people who, despite the loss of their loved one, handle it with quiet grief and acceptance and continue to take care of others.

The more grown-up you are, the more self-control you will show.

It is of immense help if you have caring people to look after you, feed you, let you know that you have support, and help you to get through this. They are there if you want to talk. They are nearby if you want to be silent.

And you need time! Somehow you have to survive one day after another as all your energy is being used to heal the mind and body

Do not forget to take care of your other children at this time.

Later Reactions

You are so lonely.

You may become depressed. You may feel that life is no longer worth living.

You may be overcome with guilt

Illnesses may become more pronounced when a loved one dies.

You may become permanently withdrawn.

You may resign from your position and retire from work.

You may become angry at the innocent baby whose birth caused your wife to die. You completely ignore the fact that it was you who caused his birth!

Is that fair?

Instead of being grateful that you have other children, you neglect them and cause them pain.

What will you do if they, too, die?

Your heart aches so much. There is this big void that is so difficult to fill, and yet, somehow, you must go on until your time comes and you can join your loved one again.

Yes, life makes no sense. One cannot understand how this tragedy happened. But there are some things you can know. Understand that your loved one did not turn into "nothing" after death. He is very much present in the other world. He can see you, even if you cannot see him. You will feel him at times. Talk to him.

For the next couple of weeks, pray for him daily. Pray that he may have peace and be surrounded by your love.

And pray for yourself. Pray that you may receive comfort and strength.

There is comfort in knowing that you will meet him again, but in the meantime, you have to handle the painful present.

He could not help dying, but you can help how you live.

Second, understand that grief can make you selfish. All you want to do is to focus on your grief. You refuse to let peace and joy come back into your life, even when three months have passed. You are neglecting your duties to yourself and others.

But peace and joy have to be deliberately put into your life. You have to seek them from within. You can do this daily by quietly spending half an hour by yourself as you think about acceptance, gratitude for what you have, and the time you had with him.

You can also appreciate the present. You may die soon too.

You can also get peace when you live in a manner that would make the deceased proud of you.

One of the biggest comforts can come from communing with nature. You can go for a walk. But note, you can get no benefit if you walk while listening to talks or music, or are on your cell phone.

You need a purpose. One purpose can be that you decide to live in a manner that would make the deceased proud of you.

The deceased needs peace too.

Your loved one, though dead, needs peace too. He cannot have peace if he looks down and sees you in emotional turmoil.

For his sake, and your own sake, it is vital that you get control over your emotions.

CHAPTER 18: HOW DO YOU HEAL?

Acknowledging the pain and crying with it is the first step in dealing with the pain. Cry alone and cry with people. It is therapeutic. This will be off and on for a long time.

We can get our strength from the love of the people around us, but we have to be open to this love.

The energy previously used in daily activities is now being consumed in handling your grief. Your grief has paralyzed you. This is okay for a short time, a few weeks, months, or so.

1. You need to be still to process your grief.

Do not go running around changing your home, remodeling, or going on a cruise.

2. Time is the greatest healer. Time will remove the sharpness of the pain.
3. Your mind has been under severe strain. It helps when it does not think of pain for some time every day.

Your mind needs to rest to sustain the heavy burden it is carrying. "When your hands get tired of carrying a heavy load, and you stop and rest them, you can lift the weight again" (Steiner). The same is true of your mind. Rest and refresh your mind by reading, going out with friends, watching a movie, listening to the news, or engaging in an absorbing activity.

4. You heal when you go for a quiet walk but you should not be on the phone.

For nature to heal, you must be open to it without distractions.

This means there is to be no phone, no one to chat with, and no music or talks to listen to while you walk. Open yourself to nature, and you will be comforted.

5. The goal of handling one day at a time will help the healing.

6. Routine is healing.

After the period of being still, you heal when you discipline yourself to follow a daily routine of things to do. There should be a fixed time to get up daily, work, eat, and exercise. Have a routine, especially when you do not want to. Force yourself to just go through the motions even when you do not want to do anything. As you keep doing so, you will begin to get stronger inside.

As changes take place in the home, and as you go about doing the day-to-day things, you heal and accept life's flow.

You, yourself, do not know how much time you have left on this earth.

One of the saddest things is watching a person become bitter with grief, not realizing that her death is just around the corner.

There is no time limit for your grief to start easing. It may take less than a year or over some years. It depends on different things and varies with different people. You do not need a grief counselor because of this.

You need a grief counselor only if, after three months, you are still immobilized and unable to function, if you do not have good friends, relatives, or a priest to talk to, and if you do not have faith in God to sustain you.

CHAPTER 19: THE "DO-NOTS" OF GRIEF

The following are behaviors that can be present in different degrees in all aspects of grief, but they are not the right way to behave. Wisdom is to overcome them and come into control. Handling grief is a life skill that should be acquired before adulthood.

From childhood, we have to learn that death is part of life and must be accepted, not fought against or escaped from.

Do not numb your grief.

If you turn to drinking and drugs to numb your grief, the grief does not get a chance to work through and will be prolonged. It will also come back later to hit you with a stronger force.

Your family members, who do not resort to alcohol or drugs to handle grief, are in just as much pain as you are.

Does it not show that you have not grown up yet?

Do not neglect your responsibilities.

To neglect your responsibilities to your children while you are grieving is wrong. The person we admire is the one who, with all his pain, still goes forward, fulfilling his responsibilities to those dependent on him. We know how difficult this is to do.

Do not run away.

You should work through the loss while living in the same surroundings.

Do not go on a cruise or a trip. Do not change everything in the house to handle the loss. Do not sell the house and move out immediately. This is because after you finish running away, the loss will hit you with the same severity.

The grief is inside you. You cannot run away from yourself.

Do you really think that people who are too poor to change their surroundings do not handle their grief well? They handle it better than you! If you are truly grieving, you neither know nor care how your surroundings look.

Do not make your home a mausoleum.

When your loved one dies, you are not supposed to convert your home into his mausoleum. You cannot tell people not to move anything out of its place or to keep it exactly as it was when he died. Do you insist that his pajamas should be exactly where they were that day? This is abnormal. You should not keep his clothes or shoes where they were at the time of his death and watch them every day for the rest of your life. The loved one's clothes and possessions should be either used or distributed and donated over the next three to six months, even if it is done gradually.

Is your memory of him so fragile that, by not seeing his things in the same place, you will forget him?

It is one thing to keep some items for remembrance. It is abnormal to insist that the house look exactly as it did before the death. People who live in one-bedroom homes remove the deceased one's belongings out of necessity. They do not love any less. They are in just as much pain. They do not suffer any mental damage because of this.

Your grief should not lead you down abnormal paths. Listen to those wiser than you. Your inheritance does not give you extra intelligence as to how to proceed with your loss.

Do not fight for control.

When you want things your way and dictate things, you are not grieving. You want power. The loss of your loved one does not excuse you for becoming arrogant, rude, and insulting to others.

Do not be swept away by grief.

Emotions must never be allowed to overcome us, whether they are grief, anger, fear, or bitterness. One will go into shock, not understand what is happening, and then be overwhelmed with sorrow. But another person cries over his grief and then accepts it. We must try to be in control. It helps when we accept that death is part of life and that it is not in our hands. It is okay to cry, but eventually, life has to go on.

A person who tries to live life as normally as he can, fulfilling his responsibilities, trying to distract himself and be happy again, does not feel the pain any less than the one who withdraws himself into bitterness and seclusion.

Social "Do-Nots."

One does not go around shaving the heads of widows.

Either a man or a woman can lead a normal life after the death of his/her spouse.

There is something very cruel about our society if it says that a man can be happy again after the death of his spouse. He can marry again, but a widow should be devoid of all happiness.

Only a very cruel man could have come up with this system!

A widow, like a widower, must be allowed to live life fully. She has the right to dress as she pleases, including makeup and jewelry. She has the right to play and attend parties, educate herself, hold a job, go to social functions, and marry again. Does not a man do this?

We have come into this world to get rid of cruelty!

CHAPTER 20: DO NOT BE IMPRISONED BY YOUR GRIEF

It takes nine months to create a life.

Your goal should be from two to nine months to be able to recover enough so that your grief no longer imprisons you.

This does not mean that you will not have sorrow. For some, the sorrow may be lifelong. But you will be able to carry on the activities of daily living, of laughing, and of appreciating life, despite the pain. You do not need a grief counselor as long as you have priests, friends, neighbors, and colleagues to talk to. Note that this does not include employers or employees.

Value yourself

When you value yourself just as much as you value the person you have lost, when you have your self-worth from many areas, when you remember how much you have handled on your own in life and survived, when you know that you have to come to this earth for a purpose, it is easier to handle your grief. You will get up from your fallen position and stand.

Do not freeze.

Know that, despite what has happened to you, you still have to live to the best of your ability. What do the animals do? They see their loved ones shot, mutilated, and eaten. They accept it. They know that they have to continue living to the best of their ability. They cannot freeze in time. To freeze is to lose peace. To freeze is to die.

Acceptance.

Acceptance is a significant step. Acceptance is of two things: your loss and the fact that now you are alone. Accept the cards that you have been dealt. They may range from rejection, pain, poverty, and loss to heartache. You have to handle them to the best of your ability.

Keep your Self-Worth.

When you have a loss, and stop taking care of yourself, or if you want to kill yourself, what are you telling the person who died? Are you not saying that you are worthless without him and that life was only worth living when he was in your life? How can you believe that? What has happened to your self-value and self-respect? What about your purpose in life? Did you not exist before this person came into your life, and quite happily, too? And that was based on your self-worth.

Never give another person the right to take away your self-worth and self-confidence.

Take charge of your emotions.

We have two enemies, the one without and the one within. The ones within consist of our emotions. Those who have practiced self-control and mental self-discipline come ahead.

Control your emotions to the degree that they cannot control you.

This is done by your resolve and by knowing that your brain cannot hold two thoughts at the same time. Fix a time each day when you will distract yourself by focusing on something else. Self-control is also achieved by meditation.

If every day you do what you are supposed to, *instead of what you feel like,* you become stronger.

When you have not allowed yourself in your past to go overboard in joy, you will not allow yourself to go overboard in sorrow.

Be inspired.

Be inspired by the courage of those around you who have been through similar circumstances.

Have a purpose.

Have a purpose in life. It may be to survive until your children are grown up. It may be to take care of those dependent on you or to fulfill the purpose of the One who sent you here. Since He sent you, He will give you the courage, but you have to ask for it!

Do not complicate it further.

If you value yourself and if you have self-worth, then your priority should be not to allow life to become even more complicated. This is not the time to fight, resign, or have an affair!

CHAPTER 21: BEREAVEMENT OF A SUICIDE

Grief and bereavement are dealt with extensively in this book, but in a death by suicide, there are some notable differences from other situations.

Regardless of what these are, the deceased must be given the same type of rituals and cremation/burial as a non-suicide would get in his family.

Suicide is dealt with extensively in a book by the author called, "Emotional Pain Versus Suicide."

The additional effects of suicide

1. Shock

The total unexpectedness of this parallels that of death by an accident except for one fact: This was planned, and yet no warning was given to the ones who cared the most.

2. Guilt.

Guilt for not picking up any sign immediately:

Hints had been given that were ignored. There was a phone call earlier that we presumed was an innocent one. Or, in our hurry, we did not wonder at the tone, or the paucity of the words, or the way the goodbye was spoken.

Guilt for not picking up signs earlier:

We did not see this coming.

We pushed him too far in his studies.

We did not pay attention when he said he was unhappy.

We were only interested in having him do what we wanted.

We did not teach him to handle the difficult times in life.

We did not give him self-worth, self-value, and self-confidence.

We could not prevent him from falling into bad company or using drugs.

3. Shame.

We withdraw from society. "What must people be thinking about us?"

4. Neglect of other children.

We are so focused on the deceased that we do not realize that our other children, too, can commit suicide! This has happened!

5. Anger at the deceased.

We have anger at them for being selfish and not thinking about the pain and welfare of others.

One must admit that suicide is a selfish act!

Lack of peace.

You may have been the cause of the suicide, or you may not have. The fact remains that the deceased is not at peace, and you are not at peace. If you believe the deceased to still exist in another realm, then it is vital to help him find peace. The fact that he does exist is comforting. This is why people attend seances.

Find peace for yourself and the dead.

Understand that the deceased left the earth, not in peace, but in emotional turmoil. He needs peace. He can see the pain that he has caused to those he left behind but is now powerless to do anything about it. When he looks down and sees you in emotional pain, he cannot have peace either. For his sake and your own sake, you must get control of your emotions.

You will also be able to handle it if you consider this as part of your destiny but note the danger.

This can be dangerous when you have other children. One should search for the causes of this suicide. If it is in the "family dynamics or the emotional makeup of the family," then there is a danger of *another* suicide in the making. An example is the inability to have good relations with others because of poor control of emotions.

Prayer gives strength. Say any prayer. You can also say the prayer outlined in the chapter, " After Death."

Remember that "it is in giving that we receive." Donations in cash or kind do comfort.

To your children, you say,

Do not overwhelm yourself with guilt.

You cannot control another person's action, only your reaction, whether in failure or rejection.

Everyone is given good times and bad times. It is how we handle the bad times that show our strength. I hope that you understand that you have come here to develop. This you can only do by handling well the different scenarios that life throws at you.

I hope that you will stay away from drugs and bad company.

I hope that you will value life.

I hope you know that I value you.

You should value yourself and your "Seven Healths," and "Fifteen Selves."

You can only become strong through control of your emotions and self-discipline."

PART 8: BE STRONG

CHAPTER 22: YOUR MANTRA

I did not ask for this type of life, but it has been given to me. Therefore, I must live it in the best way I know how.

I have to handle my pain one day at a time.

My brain is overwrought, and I need to refresh it periodically by distraction or meeting others so that it can work again.

My body is overwrought, and I need to rest it daily.

I have to handle my life one day at a time.

I have to value myself as much as I value the departed.

I have to value the rest of my family. Who knows if they will be taken away from me tomorrow?

I have to nourish and protect myself as well as those dependent on me.

I need shelter over my head and money in my hands.

I need to have work skills and financial skills.

I must not give up my job. I will support myself. I will not be a burden on society. I will work hard and save money.

I have to educate my children.

Check your access to financial, work, family, social and spiritual support.

CHAPTER 23: WHERE DO YOU GET YOUR STRENGTH?

It is never through drugs. They block the pain, but the pain is not processed.

It is never through alcohol. It blocks the pain, but the pain is not processed.

We get it from our beliefs.

We get it from our inner core.

We get it from our faith.

We can get our strength from others as we watch them handle life.

We can get our strength from God if we ask for it.

We get our strength from "time," the great healer.

It is also "in giving" that we receive strength. When we help others, we are helped.

We can get our strength from the love of the people around us, but we have to be open to the love and not harden our hearts.

It is by turning outward that we are helped.

It is never by freezing into ourselves. It is okay to grieve privately for some time, but it is self-destructive to become socially withdrawn permanently.

A couple had two children who died in their teens within a year of each other. The wife froze. She was filled with bitterness. She could not function. Her husband grieved but went on, not only with his life but also helping others. Who do you think eased his sufferings?

You, yourself, do not know how much time you have.

Acknowledge that you may die within the next year too. One of the most tragic situations is that the relative does not realize that death is not far away from him as well. He wastes his final year on this earth being sad, lonely, and bitter.

How would you live if you had only one year left?

After the time of being paralyzed by sorrow, the following will help.

Physical exhaustion will heal you. Engage in activities that will exhaust and distract you, even if it is scrubbing the floor.

When you busy yourself **by taking care of others,** you will heal.

Having a routine will help.

It helps to take care of animals and to have pets (always have them in twos). They distract you and love you for yourself.

Work helps and passes the time. If you are ready to return to work, healing will gradually come with the distraction and absorption of work. This is regardless of whether it is in your home or your career.

Take care of your social health. Try to have weekly meetings with your friends.

Do not have affairs during this mourning period.

You will also heal when you become absorbed in doing something in the name of the deceased.

You have only two choices: Allow healing to take place or destroy yourself and others around you by pain.

In the olden days, people wore black or white in mourning. This was important. If you wore your mourning colors, you not only showed respect for the deceased, but people knew you were stressed out and still emotionally distressed. They knew that you were trying to process your grief. They were more understanding, patient, comforting, and sympathetic. They knew not to overburden you and to speak appropriately. We have thrown this custom out and invited more stress. Wearing mourning colors for three months makes sense unless you are employed in a place that requires a uniform. But you can still wear an armband.

It is not wrong to be happy again after your loved one has died and you have been given the time to heal. You are not helping the deceased by being sad. That is the purpose of a mourning period. You are then set free to go on. You release yourself to go forward and live again. You need happiness to handle life. The alternative is total despair!

Your life was given to you, not to squander it in self-destructive acts. Maturity is to acknowledge the pain but then look outward and live again. Believe that you will meet again with your loved one.

CHAPTER 24: FACE YOUR DEATH

Death is a milestone, a crossroad, if you will. Death can cause spiritual growth. But it can also cause you to turn away from God. The choice is yours. Some great souls know when they are going to die, or they can postpone their death. The rest of us cannot, but at least we can be prepared.

A life without insight into one's actions, without following moral rules of absolute fairness, caring, compassion, and to "do unto others as you would have them to do to you," a life without self-control, and a life full of cruelty, anger, arrogance, greed, lust, addiction and of laziness is a life wasted! To have sorrow after such a life is justified.

But for others, death must be accepted as part of life.

This chapter is not for those who die suddenly. The heart stopped. They had an accident. They were shot. There was no time to prepare.

But what if you know that you are going to die? You have only the following choices. You can be in denial, or you can have acceptance.

It is a real fear to some people that they will dissolve into nothing after death. There is enough evidence to prove that this is not true.

Some are fearful of the possible pain as they die. There are enough medications to make you comfortable.

Some are fearful of the unknown realm that they will enter. But they are going back from where they came.

You can be in sorrow at your death or for those you leave behind. You can be angry at God and everyone else. You can be depressed since you feel powerless. But these remove clarity of vision.

When you cannot control an event, you can only control your reaction to it.

Acceptance and knowledge are the two most important things one can have.

Accept the fact that you are dying.

Have the knowledge that you are stepping into another world and are not alone as you do so.

Not one person at the time of death spoke of his wealth or status. But they were all afraid of the time they cut corners or hurt someone. Think about that.

CHAPTER 25: THE MORAL RIGHTS OF A CHILD

Should both parents risk death?

Couples who wish to serve in the defense forces of their country, or for a cause, should know that moral rights always supersede one's wishes.

It is the moral right of a child to have his parent beside him in his helpless and formative years.

This is irrespective of whether the child is a boy or a girl. You are abandoning your duties as a parent, which is a crime in itself.

If you wish to do so, why did you have a child?

If you had a child, why are you abandoning your responsibilities towards him?

No animal abandons its responsibilities to its young.

Yet we feel that we have the right to give birth to a child and then hand him over to others to raise while we go and do whatever we feel like doing!

Abnormal behavior cannot be considered normal. Society then pays the cost of this by having angry young people with no attachment and no sense of responsibility.

Who created them? You did!

This is not about doing what you feel like. This is about doing your moral duty.

Should you, the mother, volunteer your life in the services of your cause or country when you have a child who is not an adult?

The answer is "No." The father alone must serve in the defense forces.

The death of a parent has a very traumatic effect on a child with life-long scarring and handicap. To a mother, it must be said, "If you wanted to have a sense of glory and risk your life for your country, you should not have created a child. But once you do, he becomes your moral responsibility, and your first duty is to him. You, as the mother, should stay with him.

Should the father stay with the child and the mother go to fight?

The answer is "No"!

In this present time of fights over equality, we have forgotten that men and women are NOT created equal by God. They are different. The man does not have ovaries or a womb. It is the woman who has been given this gift. The woman is physically and biologically created as a nurturer.

The woman's nurturing is critical in the first fourteen years of a child's life.

You, as a woman, were created to carry the child before its birth and to nurture it after its birth. Your genes are that of a woman, and so are your responsibilities.

People who protest and come up with examples of the nurturing male must understand that in generalizing a rule, one does not look at exceptions but what is best for the child.

But, if the mother dies, the father must not serve in the armed forces. It is the moral right of the child to have his remaining parent.

This should be made legal.

Moral rights always supersede one's wishes.

PART 9: LEGAL ASPECTS OF DEATH

CHAPTER 26: A POWER-OF-ATTORNEY

"A Power of attorney" should never mean that someone takes over your whole life and you lose all your freedom. That is happening nowadays as the one who has the "power-of-attorney" decides who can come to your house, which relative or friend you should meet, whether you should live with a caretaker whom you hate, and how much money you can have. You are not allowed to choose or make decisions. People live in your home against your wishes. All quality of life is gone!

The following two points should be noted.

A power of attorney can be changed whenever you wish.

Do not choose a family member as your power of attorney.

Try not to choose a family member as your power of attorney. If he disagrees with other family members, he may prevent them from seeing you as a show of his power. Also, the other family members may not help you when you need them because they do not want to break the family dynamics. So, it is far better to choose an outsider who can also be neutral and objective.

When you choose a power of attorney, you must specify the following in writing:

The attorney can only decide that your directives and wishes are carried out and that your bills be paid. Once chosen, a power of attorney is not written in stone so that no one can question him or replace him. He has to be transparent. He can be told to meet your doctors, and his decision can be reviewed. If the doctor feels that he is too controlling, then the doctor should be able to request a new power of attorney for the welfare of his patient. You have the right to change your power of attorney whenever you want, as long as your doctor can decide that you are mentally competent.

The attorney cannot control your social life or living arrangements. He cannot decide that certain friends and relatives cannot visit you or that you cannot visit them. He has to agree that you have a right to call your relatives, and when they come, they can meet you alone without the caretaker or the attorney being present.

He cannot say that you are too incompetent to walk out of your home when you wish. Only your doctor can decide this. He cannot say that your caretaker will decide whether you can go out of the house or come down the stairs in your home. He cannot imprison you in your home. He cannot prevent any relative or friend from visiting you or taking you out to lunch or dinner, or taking you to her home. He cannot prevent you from deciding to live with a relative of your choice.

The power of attorney should never mean that only the attorney can know your diagnosis. He is there to make decisions, but you have a right to choose anyone else to share this information. You should always have one or more persons of your choice beside him to share this information. And you can change this decision anytime by letting your doctor know. This other person should not be a close relative or friend of the attorney. He cannot prevent other relatives from learning about your medical status, your diagnosis, or what treatment you are receiving. How else will someone else learn that you are not receiving adequate treatment if the attorney replaces your doctors with people whom he chooses?

The attorney cannot change your doctor without your permission. He cannot say that it is more convenient to have another doctor see you. You have to agree to have a different doctor. You should do so in the absence of the attorney and the presence of your doctor and a witness or a notary.

If the family doctor insists, the attorney must make arrangements for you to see him.

The attorney cannot fire your doctor and replace him with another unless he can prove your doctor guilty of malpractice or show evidence that your current doctor is incompetent. Your doctor has the right to see how you are doing and what your needs are, and to change your attorney if he feels you are not being treated adequately by appealing to the court. Your doctor can ask for a review by another doctor who can protest the highhandedness of the attorney to a court and ask for a change.

The attorney must keep you financially independent. He must make sure that you have a fixed amount of cash monthly, decided by you and your doctor or the court.

If the attorney does not check on you or does not appoint someone to check on you every week or when you become helpless, then he loses the right to be your power of attorney.

CHAPTER 27: ORGAN DONATION

To donate his body part is the greatest gift a person can give to someone. You donate your eyes, and someone can see. You donate your heart or other organs, and someone can live. Because of you, another person walks on this earth and can fulfill his lifespan. A family is kept intact.

Truly you have the power to give the gift of life.

But, in return for this great gift, it is to be clearly understood that:

First, the body of the person donating his organs must be treated with the *deepest respect*.

Second, the relatives be given *ample time* to say farewell to their dead beloved.

Third: the relatives must not be hurt again and again *by sending them reminders* of the death.

If this is not done, why would anyone donate?

The Tragic Scenario

The loved one, full of sorrow, with respect for the deceased's wishes, and out of caring for humanity, gives the much-beloved body of his relative for organ donation. But what follows can be terrible.

There is no time to say goodbye.

The relatives are not given any chance to say goodbye. The body is suddenly and quickly whisked away from them while they are still standing in shock.

Even while donating an organ, the relatives need the same opportunity of saying goodbye as they would have if the organs were not being donated.

Even if the body has been donated to science, the hospice nurse cannot just call "the organ people" the moment the person dies and have the body whisked away. This is inhumane. The relatives just saw their loved one die, and now the body is gone, and they were not even given time to say goodbye.

Children or immediate relatives of the deceased, coming from another country, are not given time to embrace their loved ones and say goodbye.

No one takes care of the relatives.

There is no one to greet the family and take them inside. They come to find that the body of their parent, spouse, or child has already been cut apart! What a horrible situation.

The body is desecrated.

The body is desecrated. It is cut open and left naked on the stretcher in the morgue. It is covered with blood and fluids. No one has cleaned the body. There is no sheet to cover the body.

Somebody took out the eyes for donation, and now the relatives see gaping holes where the eyes of their beloved were. No one had the decency to put artificial eyes there. No one bothered to wait until the relatives could see the deceased with his eyes intact. Blood and fluids are pouring down the face from the sockets. No one bothered to clean the face.

Promises are not kept.

The organ network people promised not to remove the skin from the chest and the abdomen, yet they have done so. Blood and fluids are pouring down the chest so that the relatives cannot embrace the deceased. Tissues and muscles lie exposed in the gaping hole.

The relatives are traumatized for life. Would you like to see your mother, child, father, spouse, or any relative in this manner? What happened to the dignity of the dead?

No one takes responsibility.

No apology is made for this. The "organ network workers" have disappeared. You cannot find out who took the body, who removed the organs, and who desecrated your loved one's body. Now, if you had not donated the organs, you would have had your loved one's body treated decently and with respect. The "organ people" did not care to make the process smooth, considerate, and respectful.

But now they want to send you letters.

From then on, every month, the letters start coming from the network, ostensibly to thank you. Why is one thank-you letter not enough? Where were they when you needed them? Why are they reviving your painful memories every month without asking permission??

Donations of vital organs are important and save lives, but until the network learns to handle people and their deceased relatives with decency, respect, and sensitivity, and until laws are put in place to protect the relatives and the body, all donations should be stopped.

The following laws are needed.

1. You cannot be forced to donate an organ.
2. Your card should allow you to mark whatever organ you wish to remove.
3. You have the right to change your mind at any time and get another card.
4. No organ will be removed until the immediate family has seen the body and given permission to take away the body, even if the driving license or the will has permission for donation.
5. If the body is donated to science, it cannot be immediately whisked away. The people who will take the body must negotiate with their loved ones about the time of their arrival.
6. The relatives or friends have the right to stay with the body, grieve over it, and then release it, even after three hours, unless the organ cannot survive.
7. It is the right of the relatives who are making such a noble sacrifice to have as much time as possible with the deceased and have the body treated with respect.
8. The people who come to collect the organs must be responsible for keeping the body clean and covered. They must be available to talk to the relatives and take them in to view the body.

9. The network people must first give you a form signed by them.

   a. The form must have the name and phone number of the person who has the responsibility for organ removal and care of the body.

   b. The form must clearly state what they will be removing. If the network people take any organ besides what you marked, they can be prosecuted.

10. The relatives cannot be approached in the first hour of death unless this was agreed to prior to the death or if the organ will be damaged. The family is undergoing enough pain. They have to be given a chance to grieve with the whole remains of the body of their loved one.

11. The body's organs cannot be removed if the immediate family is coming from overseas unless it is a vital organ that may get destroyed. Even then, the body must be cleaned up after the removal, covered with a sheet, and then returned for viewing.

12. If a vital organ cannot wait that long, the body will still stay with the available relatives for as long as possible, and they are allowed to embrace him. Then the body will be removed for a short period of time. The organ that cannot wait will be removed, but the rest will stay inside especially the eyes. The body will be stitched up neatly, cleaned, draped, and brought back to the mortuary where the relatives can see it. Other organs can be removed later.

13. Gaping holes cannot be left where the eyes had been. Eyes will be removed after the relatives have been with the body. Or, artificial eyeballs of the same color must be placed after the removal, and this is the responsibility of the network people.

14. There will be no blood or fluids running from the areas from which skin has been removed, and no tissues underneath will be exposed. Rubber leggings will be placed to absorb the fluids. Skin can only be taken from areas not exposed.

15. The whole body must be clean and covered with fresh sheets in a way that the relatives can embrace the body and kiss it.

16. There will be a representative from the organ network available until all the members have seen the body, including those who have come from far away.

17. The network should send out only one "thank-you letter" immediately after the donation. There should be no monthly or annual reminders.

CHAPTER 28: ADVANCE DIRECTIVES

It is good to make your wishes known as far ahead as possible. If you know how much you want the doctors to do and what you do not wish to be done, it gives guidelines to the doctors. It causes less pain for your loved ones. There is less guilt and less in-fighting.

Even if you do not have the formal forms or an attorney, you should be able to have your wishes written out, witnessed by two people who should not inherit anything from you, and be confirmed by a notary. Make sure that you do this in your handwriting, as the court sometimes will not accept typed documents.

My Advance Directives.

To be alive is my ability to laugh, cry, interact with others, make decisions for myself, move at least some of my body parts, and be aware of my environment and react to it.

Therefore, should I be unable to speak or make decisions for myself, I want my wishes to be followed as outlined below.

IF I HAVE NO PULSE OR AM NOT BREATHING

( ) Please do cardiac resuscitation (electric shocks by machine) to bring me back to life and intubate me. You may do dialysis.

( ) Please do **not** do Cardiac resuscitation. Do **not** put me on a respirator.

( ) Do **not** put me on dialysis.

( ) Allow my natural death.

IF I HAVE A PULSE OR AM BREATHING BUT AM UNCONSCIOUS

( ) I want full treatment with all the medical and surgical interventions to support life. This includes CPR (resuscitation to revive my heart and breathing), artificial feeding, intubation, and dialysis.

( ) I want full treatment with all medical and surgical interventions to support life. This includes CPR (electric shocks to revive the heart, respirator), artificial feeding, and dialysis, but only for the number of days as stated under the section "HOW LONG."

( ) I do not want full treatment with medical and surgical interventions to support life. This includes CPR, respirator, and dialysis.

( ) Allow my natural death but keep me comfortable.

( ) Do not feed me by making a hole in my stomach (PEG).

( ) You can make a hole in my stomach and feed me through it (PEG).

( ) You cannot feed me from anywhere except intravenously or through nasogastric tubes.

( ) Do not give me food via a nasogastric tube unless there is a chance of my recovery in the next seven days.

( ) I can be given antibiotics.

( ) Do not give me antibiotics.

( ) Do not do any more tests.

( ) You can give me fluids intravenously.

( ) You can only give me fluids through my mouth. These are to be given even if I cough. Water is not to be withheld from me.

HOW LONG?

( ) I am to be kept intubated on the respirator and dialysis for only ____ (fill in a number here, e.g., seven) days or weeks.

( ) I can be kept on the respirator if the doctors believe that I can recover or come back to my senses in the next two to three days or weeks.

( ) The respirator is to be stopped if, after ____ (fill in a number here) days, I still have a very slow pulse. Do not use medication to speed up my pulse.

( ) **The respirator is not to prolong my dying process.** Its sole purpose is to make me recover. Once two doctors have signed that there is no chance of my recovery, I am to be taken off the respirator and dialysis.

A surrogate appointed by me can only make decisions on the topics not mentioned above.

I DO NOT WISH TO PROLONG MY DYING PROCESS:

I do not wish to prolong my dying process. I do not wish, in my last few days or hours, to be tied to a

bed, tubes, or machines, including a respirator. I do not wish to be kept alive by medications or machines.

I have a right to be free of all this and go with dignity to meet my Maker.

THEREFORE,

I, _____(fill in your name), direct that all life-sustaining procedures be **withheld** in the following cases:

( ) I suffer a cardio/pulmonary/renal/multi-organ failure with no chance of recovery.

( ) I have a stroke.

( ) I become permanently unconscious.

( ) I am in a coma for _____ (fill in a number) days.

( ) I develop an irreversible illness.

( ) I develop mental deterioration.

( ) I am brain-dead.

( ) I can only live only as long as I am on drugs, machines, or by enforced feeding.

( ) I have a terminal illness.

My Wishes:

( ) I wish/ **do not** wish for any transplantation.

( ) I wish to be fully alert until my last breath, so do not sedate me.

I do not want morphine to hasten my death under the pretext that I am grimacing with pain. Only in the case where I am in severe pain and crying out, do I want pain medication.

( ) I want to have access to pain medication.

( ) I prefer to die at home unless the burden is too much for my family.

( ) I wish to be buried.

( ) I wish to be cremated.

( ) My ashes should be kept in the crypt.

( ) My ashes should be put in a river or sea.

PART 10: THE MEDICAL PROFESSION

CHAPTER 29: HOW SHOULD A DOCTOR INFORM A DEATH?

Pending Death

Do not inform a patient of a terminal illness or a grave prognosis unless he has someone with him.

First, he will not hear you completely. He has gone into shock. Second, he may have an accident on his way home.

How should the medical profession inform the patient's relatives of his impending death? The doctor should not just come in and tell the relatives that their loved one is going to die and then walk away. He should address this in three ways: the patient, the relatives, and the patient with the family.

He should talk to the patient alone and allow him to think of any questions that he will later answer.

He should later bring the relatives to a separate room and sit down and have them sit down. There should be drinking water in the room. His attitude should be one of compassion. He should explain to them that the disease is relentless and there is not much more that he can do. He should acknowledge that there are always miracles but that, in his experience, this disease does not have a cure.

Then he should sit silently for about five minutes as the relatives digest this terrible news. He then answers questions, after which he lets the relatives stay in the room while he leaves, saying that they can contact him later if they wish.

He should ask a nurse to go in after about fifteen minutes, check on the relatives, and answer further questions. The nurse must be compassionate and patient.

The relatives can speak to him again later, but they should have only one spokesperson and not meet him individually. They can forward their list of questions to this person.

One of the questions he may have to answer is whether the patient can go home to spend his last few days in familiar surroundings or if there is too much medical equipment needed.

He should also talk to the patient and the family together. Then they can leave.

When you, the doctor, have just told someone in your office that he will die in a fixed time, do not leave him outside to sit with the other people in the reception room as you ponder your next move. He should sit in a separate room alone, and then one of your workers should check on him.

This is not the time to ask him to wait in your office while you do blood tests. The person is in shock. He needs time to digest what he has heard. Bring him back another time to have the tests unless he has come from far away. Do not let him drive. Arrange for a taxi or someone to pick him up. Be very sure before you give him your verdict.

If the patient asks the doctor about whether he is going to die, he should be told the truth. The only exception to this is if the patient is very nervous, and the doctor feels that he will be overcome with anxiety.

But most of us would like to know how much time we have left on this earth so that we can make whatever arrangements we have to make and fulfill our last wishes. Even the condemned man in prison is given this much compassion.

Do not think that by telling him you will hasten his death or cause a heart attack. People handle the news of their demise fairly well. How many heart attacks have you seen among the people you have told or among the persons condemned to death? Usually, the patient knows, but it is closer to the end.

On the other hand, if he is fearful of death, or in a state of denial, there is no need for you to force him to acknowledge the fact. People do not have to be told if they cannot handle it, and you will sense this, but the family should be told. If a person states that he will get well, acknowledge the possibility. We all know that miracles do happen.

If a death has occurred.

If the patient has died, the doctor brings the family to a room as described above and speaks to them in the same way. The doctor sits silently for five minutes as the family digests the news. After this, he expresses his sympathy and leaves.

What the doctor does not do is merely say that he is sorry and leave.

Neither does he tell the nurse or a junior physician to break the news. He has to break the news. This is compassion on your part as the doctor. This shows that you care. The only exception is if the doctor is overwhelmed with multiple deaths.

It is maturity on the relative's part to hear this without shouting and fighting unless there has been an act of malpractice. Do not follow the behavior shown on television!

Even though emotions are running high, the relative needs to keep calm to see what else should be done. What he does not do is shout at the doctor and attack him!

On hearing the news, the relative should be silent at first to let the news sink in and then ask his questions.

> The more self-control he shows, the better he will be able to handle the grieving process.

Mutual respect on both sides (the doctor and the relative) will go a long way to make this encounter less traumatic.

CHAPTER 30: CRUELTY AND THE MEDICAL PROFESSION

We expect doctors to be compassionate to the dying as well as the living. Medical colleges are supposed to send forth compassionate doctors! But think about the following.

From the first day that a student enters a medical college, he is expected to commit cruelty or witness cruelty without caring to stop it or be affected by it. This then qualifies him to be considered a scientist. He is to watch helpless animals caged, allowed no freedom, and repeatedly tortured in the name of science. He must not protest! If he flinches, he is treated with contempt by his professors!

Acid is placed in the eyes of the animals. They are cut without anesthesia or burned. Needles are inserted into their brains. They are forced to run on treadmills while fluids leak from their surgical wounds and cables hang from their bodies. The teachers force the students to do repeated surgeries on the animals so that the doctors can practice their skills *without one thought of the pain that the animals are suffering.*

The animals are forced to stand in contorted positions for hours. They are burned to see how they handle the pain afterward and what pain medications work, and the students watch impassively while the animals writhe in pain.

What sort of a human being can do this? Certainly not a compassionate one! Can you do this? This is a course in sheer cruelty.

When a student protests or is unable to do so impassively, he is looked upon with contempt by his teachers and said to be weak. So, he keeps doing this until he has become completely hardened to expressions of pain. He has become heartless.

And now he gets to treat you.

After five years, he is released to the public and told to be a compassionate doctor! Does that make sense? Is that possible? Very few people can go through this without profoundly changing. How can he be a compassionate doctor? Your screams of pain will only reflect the screams of the animals that he tortured in his studies.

He has been brainwashed to not be affected by these screams. The brain cannot miraculously change and say, "I will not be affected by the screams of the animals that I am torturing, but I will drown in compassion when a human is crying."

If the scream of a tortured, frightened animal cannot affect him enough to move to stop its pain, how can the scream of a patient in pain?

Those who think this is possible have buried their heads in the sand. Do not the guards in prison become hardened to the screams of the inmates? Why do we recoil when we are told about Hitler's people experimenting on people?

To the human brain, a scream in pain is a scream from any living being, whether an animal or a human.

A doctor cannot be a "Jekyll and Hyde" person. He cannot turn his reaction to another's suffering off and on. If he were a Jekyll and Hyde personality, you would not want him as your physician!

What human being is able to do such cruelty? And yet this is done in all the medical colleges, including famous institutions such as the Mayo Clinic. It is not only the pharmaceutical companies that torture animals.

When a person knows that what he is doing is wrong, he keeps it a secret.

So do these medical colleges: They do not want anyone to know what they are doing. They destroy the vocal cords of the animals so you cannot hear their screams.

Tell them to allow public televisions in their laboratories. Let them allow the public to inspect their laboratories while performing experiments if they have nothing to hide.

But you, the public, are affected. Doctors are loaded on you who have forgotten what it is to be compassionate.

We learn compassion only when we see compassion around us.

And our compassion starts when we treat animals with compassion.

Do you not think that you deserve a truly compassionate doctor? Do you not think that one of the duties of every medical college is to produce humane doctors?

Human beings are basically very kind people. When they hear of someone torturing an animal, they recoil from him in horror!

It is your right to demand that medical and pharmaceutical laboratories shut down all types of animal torture? Just as you refuse to buy pharmaceutical products from companies that torture animals, it is now your duty to expose these colleges to protest the torture and inhumane treatment that they do to animals.

Ask medical colleges, "Do you torture animals, and if so, why?" In all these centuries, they have tortured enough animals to know their anatomy. Why do they not practice on plastic models? Why is this torture still needed today when computers can show us every aspect of the human body?

The torture of animals by medical students or doctors must be banned. No society can progress when it practices cruelty in any form, especially to helpless beings.

Thankfully, there are still some compassionate doctors who survive this.

Several thousands of them have formed an organization called "The Physicians Committee for Responsible Medicine" (PCRM) located in Washington, D.C., USA. They have successfully shut down the Medical University of South Carolina and the University of

Washington, which used live animals in their general surgery program (can you imagine the horror?). They have also stopped the Colorado University and the University of Toledo from experimenting on animals in Veterinary medicine (They torture an animal before they teach you to save it)! They have marched to the White House, but no one has listened.

This organization is open to the public for membership. And now, it is your turn to join the war against cruelty.

> Cruelty in any form is cruel, and a cruel person can never become humane.

THE END

M. Kukreja, M.D.

www.ingramcontent.com/pod-product-compliance
Lightning Source LLC
Chambersburg PA
CBHW020009050426
42450CB00005B/391